Our Lives,
Our World

Bangladesh

Chrysalis Children's Books

First published in the UK in 2004 by
Chrysalis Children's Books
An imprint of Chrysalis Books Group
The Chrysalis Building, Bramley Road
London W10 6SP

Copyright © Chrysalis Books Group Plc 2004

Compiled and edited by Susie Brooks
Editorial manager: Joyce Bentley
Designed by: Tall Tree Books Ltd
Photographic consultant: Jenny Matthews
Picture researcher: Jamie Dikomite

ISBN 1 84458 088 1

Printed in China

10 9 8 7 6 5 4 3 2 1

British Library Cataloguing in Publication Data for
this book is available from the British Library.

The Publishers would like to thank the
photographers: Monirul Alam, Andrew Biraj, Nazrul
Chowdhury and Juthi Howlader for capturing these
wonderful children on film.
Corbis: Tom Brakefield FC CR, 1B, 5B; Peter Finger
FC BL, 4TR; Roger Wood 15CR, 31CL; Reuters
30B. Rex Features: David M Hayes 5T, Sipa
Press 21CR.

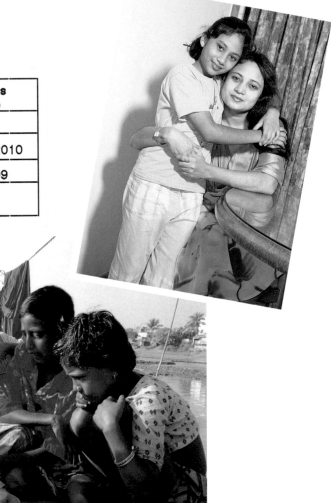

Contents

Ei je! – Hello!

We are the children of Bangladesh and we can't
wait to share our lives with you in this book!

Welcome to Bangladesh!

We've got so much to show you. Let's start by telling you a bit about our country. We hope you'll come and see Bangladesh for yourself some time soon!

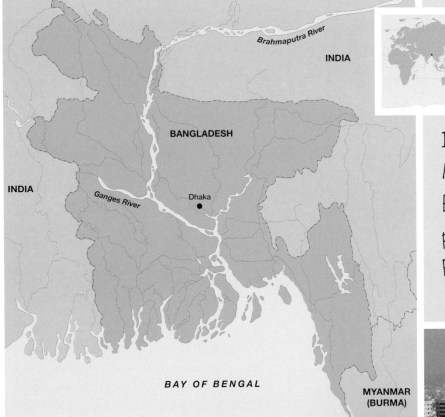

Brahmaputra River

INDIA

BANGLADESH

INDIA

Ganges River

Dhaka

BAY OF BENGAL

MYANMAR (BURMA)

Our country

Bangladesh is in Southeast Asia. It is surrounded by India, Myanmar (Burma) and the Bay of Bengal. Our country's proper name is The People's Republic of Bangladesh.

Crowded capital

Bangladesh is not a big place but it has a huge population. More than 9 million people live in Dhaka, our capital city.

The great Ganges
Many of the waterways in Bangladesh are channels of the River Ganges. They are very important to the daily lives of fishermen, farmers and many other people.

Land and climate
Hundreds of rivers wind their way through Bangladesh. Between them the land is mainly flat, with a few hilly areas in the east. Bangladesh has a tropical climate, with hot, humid summers and seasons of very heavy rain.

National flag
This is our flag. It is green, like our land, with a bright red sun.

Local nature
Our national animal, the Royal Bengal tiger, lives near the coast in swampy forests. The water lily (top left) is our national flower.

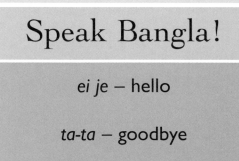

Speak Bangla!

ei je – hello

ta-ta – goodbye

doya kore – please

dhonnobad – thank you

Sashi

Hi! My name is Sashi and I am 7 years old. I live in Dhaka with my parents and my 13 year-old sister Sawrna. Our housekeeper Rujina and my cousin Rajib also stay in our flat. We live in a community close to the railway line.

'I get excited when someone tells me ghost stories!'

This is my family. My mum is called Mukul. She looks after me at home, but she works as a writer, too.

My dad, Sohrab, is a banker – he works in an office in Dhaka.

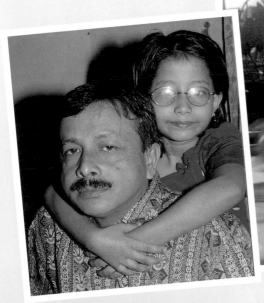

Here I am in the bedroom I share with Sawrna and Rujina. I'm playing the organ – it's one of my favourite hobbies! I like to sing along, too. One day I want to be a professional singer.

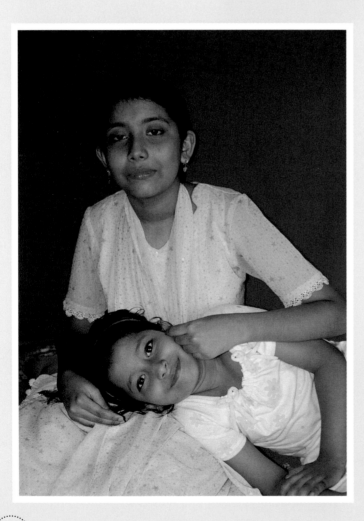

Sawrna and I get on really well. I like having an older sister – she's teaching me how to put on make-up!

This is the bathroom where I wash before I go to bed and before I say my prayers. I pray to Allah five times a day.

When I pray I kneel on my prayer mat and cup my hands.

Praying to Allah

Sashi, like most people in Bangladesh, is a Muslim. She follows a religion called Islam and she worships Allah, the Islamic god. Muslims pray to Allah at least five times a day. Sometimes they go to a mosque to do this. Before they pray, they have to wash their face, hands and feet.

I've been taking dancing lessons since I was 4. My bracelets and ankle bells mean that when I move, my movements become part of the music. I practise at home, but the jingling sound gets on mum's nerves!

My school is not far away. I travel there in this pedalled school van. There are 65 of us in my class. My friends and I like to mess around after lessons!

My school teacher is called Aprin. She is very kind to us all.

Traditional costume

The wrap-around costume that Sashi's teacher wears is called a 'sari'. It is the traditional clothing for Bangladeshi women. Another traditional outfit is the 'salwar kameez' – a collarless tunic worn over loose trousers. Boys and men dress mainly in Western-style clothing or pyjama-like suits, but some wear the 'lungi' – a long piece of material, wrapped around like a skirt.

Juvoraz

Hello, I'm Juvoraz! My name means prince, but I don't have a castle – I live on a boat on the Turag river near Dhaka. I am 10 years old and I have three younger brothers and an older sister. We all share the boat with our parents.

'I want to have a good job, so that one day I can look after my family.'

Our house boat is part of a community of floating people. We are known as gypsies.

Here I am on the boat with my brothers – Omor Sani, aged 5, Shahrukh Khan, who's 3, and Sindbad who is 8 years old.

Omor Sani

Shahrukh Khan

Sindbad

I have a pet, too – a duck called Raz. Ducks are my favourite animals. I sometimes feed Raz scraps leftover from our meals.

13

We don't have a bathroom on the boat – we just use the river water. Sometimes in the mornings it's a bit cold, but it wakes me up!

River water

Many poor people like Juvoraz live on the rivers of Bangladesh. They move around to wherever there is work and fresh water. Drinking the dirty river water is very dangerous. People can catch deadly diseases, such as cholera, if they don't boil or filter the water first.

We also use the river for washing our clothes. Then we hang them out on the boat to dry. This is my sister Morium, washing her dress.

We have a small space for cooking on the deck of the boat. Our food is very simple. We eat rice and vegetables for almost every meal, sometimes with fish.

I help my dad prepare the fish that he buys from the market.

Rice for life

Boiled rice is eaten daily by almost everyone in Bangladesh, whether they are rich or poor. Fish, meat, vegetables and spices may be added to it, according to what the family can afford. Rice is grown in waterlogged fields called paddy fields. The flat, wet land in Bangladesh is perfect for this type of farming.

I go to school for two hours every morning except Fridays. It's an open-air school with no classroom or playground. I try to learn more by studying on the boat with my friends. My favourite subject is writing. Our language is Bangla.

Struggling to learn

Many people in Bangladesh have grown up without ever learning to read or write. The situation is improving, but it is still difficult for poor children to get a good education. In many places, schools and teachers are in short supply. What's more, children often need to take on paid jobs to help earn money for their family.

In my spare time I like diving and playing in the water. It's a good way to keep cool in the steamy summer weather!

I sleep on the floor of the boat. There are no separate bedrooms, so my whole family shares this space. It can get quite squashed in here. I'm taking a quick nap while no one else is around!

Rojena

Hi! My name is Rojena. I'm 8 years old and I live in a small house near the river in Dhaka. I have three sisters, but two of them have married and left home. I work with my family every day, breaking stones.

'When I grow up I want to be a good mother and have my own home.'

Here I am with mum, dad and my younger sister, Tulekha. We are sitting on the rocky river bank where we work. I don't go to school because I do not have time.

Stone breakers

Rojena and her family are among many poor people who are employed to break stones into small pieces. The stones are used for making roads and sometimes buildings. Many industries in Bangladesh use child workers because they will do the job for very little money.

My house is near where I work. It stands on stilts, to keep it dry when the river floods. There's only one room inside – we all sleep there together.

19

I break stones using a heavy mallet. It is hard and tiring work. I strap pieces of rubber around my feet, in case I hit them by mistake!

The men are much stronger than me. They break down the big rocks and I make them smaller. We work from early in the morning until late at night. I get paid about 25 pence per day. It's not much, but I'm glad that I am helping my family.

People carry the small stones on their heads and load them onto boats and lorries. Sometimes the lorries get stuck in the flood!

Flooding

There are floods every year in Bangladesh. They usually happen when heavy rains, called monsoon rains, fill the rivers to bursting point. Often the floods cause serious damage, swamping towns and villages, wrecking homes and farmland and even killing people.

These are some of the other workers, taking a quick break.

The heat of the sun is very strong here. Every day we each bring to work a parasol for shade, as well as a can of food. We boil the river water for drinking – I get really thirsty, but I have to make my ration last!

We stop for lunch at 1.00 pm. We usually have rice with potatoes and chilli. On special occasions we eat 'payesh', which is rice cooked with milk and sugar.

I'm hungry because breakfast was a long time ago – at 6.30 am! I sit on the floor and eat using my right hand. Sometimes I share my food with others.

Rules for eating

Rojena and her family are Muslims and their meals are guided by their religion. According to the koran, the holy book of Islam, it is polite to eat only with the right hand. Muslims should also sit with their knees raised or legs crossed, and thank Allah for their food.

Barsha

Hello, I'm Barsha! I am 12 years old and I live in Dhaka with my mum who's a teacher. My dad lives abroad in Dubai, so I don't see him much – but I often talk to him on the phone. Sometimes he sends me surprise presents!

'If I could have a wish come true, it would be to fly like a bird but without wings!'

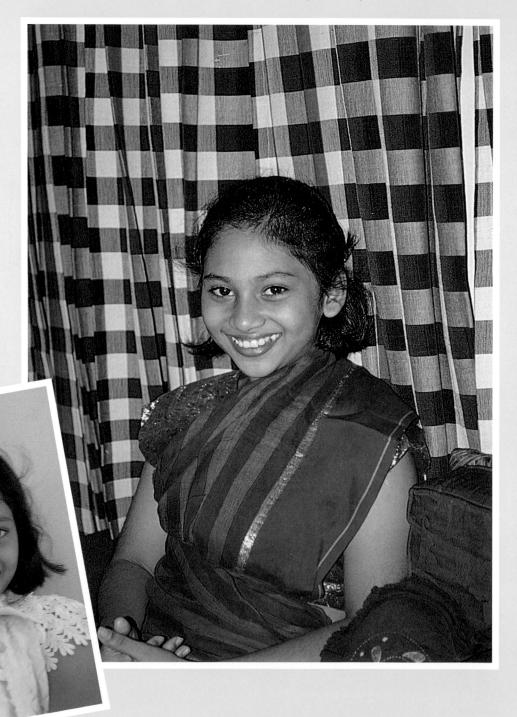

24

Here I am playing with my cousin Turza who lives nearby. I'm wearing my sari because we are ready to celebrate a Muslim festival.

Mum and I are best friends. I sometimes help her around the house. This is the entrance to our building. Inside there are three bedrooms, two bathrooms, a dining room, a drawing room and a kitchen. We have no garden but there are two balconies – one at the front and one at the back.

Barsha comes from a wealthy family and she studies at private school. She takes all her lessons in English, except Bangla and religious classes. This type of education is expensive and not many people can afford it. But those who can have a strong chance of going to university and getting a good job when they leave. Muslim children do not go to school on Fridays because that is their day of prayer.

I go to school five days a week, from Sunday to Thursday. Mum drives me there in our car. I have to get up early to be ready in time for lessons at 8.00 am. I put on the school uniform – a white shirt and blue skirt.

My classroom is on the first floor of the school building. I get on well with my teacher and I love writing on the blackboard! My favourite subject is maths because I find it really easy.

School finishes at 2.00 pm. When I'm waiting for mum to come and pick me up, I like to play basketball in the playground with my friend Sitab.

I help mum cook lunch at home – we eat at around 2.30 pm. We usually have delicious curries or dahl (spicy lentil soup) with rice.

Full of flavour

As well as rice, many spices, fruits and vegetables are grown in Bangladesh. These are often used in traditional cooking. Spicy curries made with chilli, garlic, ginger and turmeric, along with a mixure of meat or fish and vegetables, are very popular.

Sometimes, during the afternoon, we go for a trip into town. I love taking a ride on the rickshaw! I don't get pocket money, but I ask mum to buy me things when we're in the shops!

Travelling around

Rickshaws are one of the most common forms of transport in Bangladesh. They are small, pedal-driven carts which people use like taxis to get around town. In Dhaka, the streets are full of them. It is usually quicker and more convenient to take a rickshaw than a bus. For longer-distance travel, boats are popular because there are so many rivers linking places in Bangladesh.

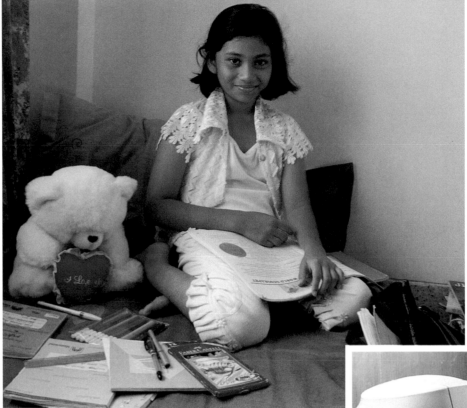

When I'm not out and about, I have to do my homework. I try to study hard because I want to be successful. I like brightening up my work by drawing pictures and colouring them in.

I sometimes practise drawing on my computer. I also use it for other schoolwork, and sometimes for listening to music. I'd like to be a computer engineer when I grow up.

In the evenings, my favourite pastime is watching TV. I like cartoons – especially Tom and Jerry – but I don't always get to watch what I want!

Our Year

Here are some important events in our calendar!

JANUARY
New Year's Day This is a day off school and work!

Barsha's birthday: 27 January

FEBRUARY
Shaheed Day We lay wreaths and remember the people who died in 1952 so that we could keep our national language, Bangla.

Eid-ul-Azha We celebrate the life of the Muslim prophet Ibrahim.

MARCH

Independence Day Guns are fired, flags are flown and buildings are lit to mark the day that Bangladesh became an independent country.

Holi Hindus spray each other with coloured water to celebrate the idea of goodness winning over evil.

Sashi's birthday: 15 March

APRIL
Bengali New Year There are parades and fairs all over the country, with traditional foods and Bangla songs.

MAY/JUNE
Mohammed's Birthday We celebrate the birthday of the prophet Mohammed, who was the first person to spread the word of Islam.

Buddha Purnima This is a Buddhist festival and a national holiday.

30

Rojena and Juvoraz don't know when their birthdays are.

AUGUST/SEPTEMBER

Janamashtami Hindus fast for a day then celebrate at midnight in honour of their god Krishna's birthday.

SEPTEMBER/OCTOBER

Shab-e-Barat We pray to the Muslim god Allah and share food and sweets with our neighbours.

Durga Puja Hindus place statues of their goddess Durga in temples and days of parades and boat races take place.

OCTOBER/NOVEMBER

Eid-ul-Fitr We wear new clothes, pray at the mosque and have parties and feasts to celebrate the end of Ramadan, a month of daily fasting.

DECEMBER

Victory Day We fly flags and watch colourful processions and street performances, in celebration of Bangladesh's victory in the 1971 war against Pakistan.

Christmas A national holiday. Christians in our country replant banana trees outside their homes and churches and light them with oil lamps.

Ta-ta! – Goodbye!

Glossary

Bangla (also called Bengali) The language of Bangladesh.

cholera A deadly disease carried by dirty water.

monsoon A season of heavy rain, driven by a strong wind.

mosque A Muslim place of worship.

Muslim A follower of the religion Islam. Most people in Bangladesh are Muslims. There are also some Hindus, Buddhists and Christians.

paddy field A field planted with rice.

salwar kameez A traditional girl's outfit, consisting of a long tunic and loose trousers.

sari A traditional women's dress, made of a very long piece of fabric, wrapped and gathered around the body.

turmeric A yellow-coloured plant, ground as a spice.

Index